Radical Notes 6

LOSS AS RESISTANCE

Towards a Hermeneutic of Revolution

Pothik Ghosh

Series Editors

Pratyush Chandra

Pothik Ghosh

Ravi Kumar

Saswat Pattanayak

LOSS AS RESISTANCE: Towards a Hermeneutic of Revolution

Pothik Ghosh

First Published, 2010

ISBN 978-93-5002-064-7

Published by
AAKAR BOOKS
28 E Pocket IV, Mayur Vihar Phase I, Delhi-110 091
Phone : 011-2279 5505 Telefax : 011-2279 5641
aakarbooks@gmail.com; www.aakarbooks.com

Printed at
Mudrak, Delhi-110 091

A movement in a sense is a struggle over the definition of reality—how reality is constituted. It is this struggle that builds the focus and targets of the movement, informing the praxes towards social transformation. Inherent in this struggle is the act of reclaiming—sense and sensibility, words and meaning...

The word "radical", which in this post-Cold War phase of Global Capitalism or globaloney has been reduced to a general notion characterizing all kinds of extremism and deviance, is one such word that has been time and again reclaimed by the practitioners of social transformation. "Radical" derived from the Latin word, 'radix' meaning 'root' = 'basic' = 'fundamental' is a concept that aptly defines a transformatory practice as an endeavour to reveal and target the essence of what is given to us in appearance. Radicalism in this sense is nothing but fundamental transformation rather than politicking in appearances. Further, and foremost, it is the all-round critique of the status quo and its genealogies, rather than accepting the disciplinary divide/boundaries that the capitalist system perpetuates in order to control labour-power and labour, our efforts and their fruits.

Radical Notes is an endeavour to coordinate the radical voices around the globe, with special focus on South Asia. In our view such focus (which could have been anything) is not just for convenience, given the facilitators' cultural and intellectual comfort, but is also needed to concretise any 'radical' pursuit. In our view South Asia provides us the opportunity to visualize the reproduction of 'global' capitalism and struggle against it in a regional setting. But we must remember such focus is always fluid with the ever-dynamic radical needs of the humanity.

Radical Notes booklets are contributions on social, cultural, political or economic issues from counter-hegemonic perspectives, which need not be confined to any established socialist and communist current of thought (though these approaches are most welcome).

Series Editors
Radical Notes

Contents

1. Loss: From Phenomenology to Structure 5
2. The Horizon of Revolution: A Dialectical Dance 12
3. The Psychoanalytic Moment of Revolution 18
4. The Free Self: Pseudo-Recovery or What? 22
5. The Symbolic Economy of Aesthetics: A Coopted Tale 25
6. Loss As Resistance: A New Constellation of Revolution 32
7. An Unlikely Communist Hero 35
8. No History Without Loss: Poetic Lessons from Nature 41
9. Future is Forever, Or How Not to Regain Lost Time 46

1

Loss: From Phenomenology to Structure

The idea of loss is, without doubt, an object of overriding concern in the canons of psychoanalysis. It also defines, as we would all know, the imaginary of what is called modernism in art and literature. But this idea of loss is perceived to have a rather un-Marxian ring to it. Can that, however, be taken as an accurate account of the relationship between loss and working-class politics, especially of a Marxian vintage? One would wish to begin exploring the theoretical plausibility of such a question by asserting at the outset, perhaps in violation of the kosher rules of dispassionately neutral academic theory, that a revolutionary politics of resistance and class struggle is not possible without a sense and consciousness of loss. That this idea of loss does not figure on the surface of the dominant discourse generated by such politics does not take away from the fact that it has always been its subterranean, constitutive field. But it is time now to foreground this inextricable link between revolutionary politics and the idea of loss in order to save such politics, and its Marxian theory and discourse, from being identified with a normative-Stalinist modality of 'revolutionary' politics. Something that both the poststructuralist detractors and communistological proponents of Marxism have been equally culpable of.

What is intended here is an attempt to foreground this relationship between loss and revolutionary politics by exploring how loss can be perceived, articulated and (re)defined within the Marxist paradigm. And in order to accomplish that one would try to come up with an abstract, philosophical model of loss, which is framed by a Marxist understanding of the totality of human experience, even as one simultaneously follows one's subjective preferences with regard to literature, art and cinema to choose, in a seemingly eclectic and random fashion, certain works that one thinks would enable the expression and explication of this critical Marxist logic of loss. Even at the risk of getting ahead of ourselves, we would do well to remember that a Marxist conceptualisation of loss no longer allows the consciousness of loss to remain as such because such a conceptualisation is bound up with the transfiguration of the sense of loss into a subjectivity of revolutionary resistance. This exploration, considering that it is being carried out under the twin-signs of working-class politics and psychoanalysis, shall naturally entail a juxtaposition, even transposition, of terms of canonised philosophy and Marxist theory with those of Freudian, especially Lacanian, psychology and psychoanalysis. This approach, which seems in the beginning to be analogical, will eventually reveal how philosophical and Marxist terminology when transposed into psychoanalytic discourse and vice-versa do not merely serve a metaphorical or allegorical function, but exhibit an underlying logical unity as well.

To better comprehend how a consciousness of loss emerges within the Marxist paradigm as a reconstituted subjectivity of struggle and resistance, we need to understand that the sense of loss as loss emerges within and due to the same logical horizon within and by which that loss is produced as an empirical fact. Thus perception of loss as loss, and the consciousness that is contingent on such perception, is an externalised perception of loss insofar as it is bound up with the same logic that has resulted in that loss and makes it *appear* so. Clearly then, the meaning of loss that is conferred on the empirically extant phenomenon of loss is inextricable from its production as an empirical actuality. It has nothing to do with the expression of how loss experiences itself. In other words, loss, whether it is ignored or recognised as loss, is a distortion of the real insofar as it is registered through a process of imposition of an external sign that robs the real of its reality by replacing it with a symbolic meaning that it is not. Thus the sense of loss, in spite of it coming into being by overcoming the oblivion which the constitutive logic of actually existing history seeks to relegate it to, is no more than the consciousness of loss as an externalised, phenomenological documentation. This consciousness of phenomenological documentation embodies the logic of objectification, which is precisely the invasive, autonomy-destroying, truth-sapping symbolic logic of capitalist modernity that has produced it as an actual, empirical fact in the first place. For loss to really become conscious of itself, it has to become the autonomous expression of its own interiority. In so doing, it will become an active subject by resisting objectification and its constitutive representational/symbolic logic to become another. It will thus cease to be loss and become what we could now call resistance.

This inversely differential relationship between two senses of loss – one passive because of its situation within the symbolic logical horizon of capitalist modernity and the other transfigured into resistance – is captured by poet-filmmaker Pasolini in 'The Weeping of the Excavator' (*Roman Poems*). The most illustrative lines are cited here:

To their neighborhoods, to their suburbs
the young return on light motorbikes –
in overall and workpants

but spurred on by a festive excitement,
with a friend behind on the saddle,
laughing and dirty. The last customers

stand gossiping with loud voices
in the night, here and there, at tables
in almost-empty still brightly-lit bars.

Stupendous and miserable city,
you taught me what joyful ferocious men
learn as kids,

the little things in which the greatness
of life is discovered in peace,
how to be tough and ready

in the confusion of the streets,
addressing another man, without trembling,
not ashamed to watch money counted

with lazy fingers by sweaty delivery boys
against facades flashing by
in the eternal color of summer,

to defend myself, to offend,
to have the world before my eyes
and not just in my heart,

to understand that few know the passions
which I've lived through:
they are not brothers to me,

and yet they are true brothers
with passions of men who,
light-hearted, inconscient,

live entire experiences unknown to me.
Stupendous and miserable city,
which made me experience that unknown life

until I discovered what
in each of us
was the world.

A moon dying in the silence that lives on it
pales with a violent glow
which miserably, on the mute earth,

with its beautiful boulevards and old lanes,
dazzles them without shedding light,
and a few hot cloud masses

reflect them over the world.
It is the most beautiful summer night.
Trastevere, smelling of straw

from old stables and half-empty wine bars,
isn't asleep yet.
The dark corners and peaceful walls

echo with enchanted noise.
Men and boys returning home
under festoons of lonely light,

toward their alleys choked with darkness and garbage,
with that light step
which struck my soul

when I really loved,
when I really longed to understand.
And now as then, they disappear, singing.

The initial lines of the excerpt can be read as Pasolini's account of what the "stupendous" and "miserable" city of Rome has taught him, the lost detritus of the actual life that Rome is, by way of surviving as that detritus. It constitutes for loss, embodied by the poet, a passive consciousness of itself. It is all about knowing how to live the life of detritus as detritus. This knowledge and its practice, and the associated consciousness, is the affirmation of the logic that produces the life of such loss-exuding jetsam while signifying it as such.

However, as we proceed further down the poem we find the poet encountering members of the Roman underclass, who, despite sharing his actual empirical condition of low life and loss, thrust upon them by the capitalist modernity of Rome, experience their lives of loss and *know* that loss in a manner that is unknown to the poet. It is this difference in the sense that each makes of their common condition of loss that we see the two different registers or consciousness of loss – loss as loss and loss becoming an active subject to be transfigured into another.

That Pasolini is able to distinguish between his phenomenological, externalised sense and register of loss from what that sense becomes when it gets transformed into its own subject, thereby ceasing to be loss, is clear when he writes:

Men and boys returning home
under festoons of lonely light,

toward their alleys choked with darkness and garbage,
with that light step
which struck my soul

when I really loved,
when I really longed to understand.
And now as then, they disappear, singing.

The "darkness" and "garbage" that he talks about indicates how the sense of loss for him resides on the surfaces of the actual fact of loss produced by his and his underclass "brothers'" empirically lived actual history and its spatio-temporality. His simultaneous longing to understand their disappearance and singing is his yearning to enter the entrails of loss to become one with loss's sense and expression of its own interiority, whereby the expression of loss becomes another, evident in the non-despairing register of singing by people who in actual, empirical history have been experiencing that loss and its despair. The disappearance of those people indicates, for Pasolini and his readers, the fleetingness with which one encounters the transfigured experience of loss-as-another when one is still caught in the passive, phenomenological and externalised experience of loss.

It is this phenomenological, externalised experience (or shall we say account) of loss that Pasolini seeks to devalue vis-à-vis another where loss is becoming the subjectivity of its own interiority:

A moon dying in the silence that lives on it
pales with a violent glow
which miserably, on the mute earth,

with its beautiful boulevards and old lanes,
dazzles them without shedding light,...

Light, when it is shed, is always an externality, whereas the "dying" of "a moon in the silence that lives on it... with a violent glow" that "dazzles..without shedding light" is an image that invokes the transfiguration of loss into another where loss ceases to be (dies) like Pasolini's moon. And in so "dying", and transfiguring, his moon of loss glows and dazzles the objects of Pasolini's Rome of loss without shedding its light on them. That implies the loss embodied by each of those objects of Rome of loss appear not in the external light that *identifies* them as loss but in their own glow, thereby ceasing to be objectified embodiments of loss to become subjective embodiments of another.

Nevertheless, the emergence of such subjectivity of resistance through the transformation of the objectified and passive consciousness of loss is, as should be fairly obvious, not possible without undergoing that experience of loss, and acquiring a passive and symbolised consciousness of loss as loss. In other words, the subjectivity of resistance – which is born out of the will and endeavour of an ontological embodiment of loss to transgress the symbolic boundary within which it is produced and signified as loss – cannot be conjured up from thin air through a voluntaristic feat. It can arise and be conceived of only as a determinate critique in and of a historically particular but logically quasi-objective and universal horizon of capitalist modernity. Pasolini is aware of that:

Stupendous and miserable city,
which made me experience that unknown life

until I discovered what
in each of us
was the world.

This, needless to say, is a rather perilous affair. To come to grips with the dangerously fraught nature of this dialectically determinate relationship between a passive consciousness of loss and an active subjectivity of resistance – or capitalist modernity and the counter-capitalist subject immanent in it – we would do well to properly grasp the architectonics of the dynamic of production of loss, loss gaining consciousness of itself as loss and its transfiguration into another.

2

The Horizon of Revolution:
A Dialectical Dance

To envisage loss/excess only in ontological terms is to reify or congeal it. This keeps loss, as its name suggests, within the horizon of capitalism – produced and articulated by its constitutive logic of contradiction, and alienated dichotomisation between gain (or victory) and loss that such competitive contradiction inevitably results in. Such ontological congealment is intrinsic to the logic of alienation (of capitalist modernity) that disrupts the process of reality by estranging its various moments from one another into isolated, struggling monads. The consciousness of congealed and ontologised loss is, thus, as much determined by the capitalist logical tendency of competition, alienation and externalised determination (domination) as the ontology of gain that originates the competitive tendency and reinforces it.

In such circumstances, to pose loss as loss, that is, as a congealed ontology, against the ontological embodiment of gain is to remain stuck within the horizon of capitalist modernity and reinforce its alienating logic. That is precisely why the consciousness of loss as a congealed ontology resonates with the politics of communitarian (or petty-bourgeois) anti-capitalism, and is the constitutive glue of Fascism and Bonapartism in the societal or statist moment of politics. It manifests itself in the realm or moment of remembrance – something that we here are more concerned about – as congealed memory or nostalgia. It is, therefore, not surprising that the Fascist historiographical mode – evident, for instance, in the Sangh Parivar's vision of history – is nostalgic. Proust's way of remembering, that is recovering memories and the loss that accompanies the transformation of lived experiences into memories, is the inverse of the nostalgic framing of memories and loss as congealed facts or entities. Benjamin explicates this impulse in 'The Image of Proust' (*Illuminations*):

"We know that in his work Proust did not describe a life as it actually was, but a life as it was remembered by the one who had lived it. And yet even this statement is imprecise and far too crude. For the important thing for the remembering author is not what he experienced, but the weaving of his memory, the Penelope work of recollection. Or should one call it, rather, a Penelope work of forgetting? Is not the involuntary recollection, Proust's memoire involontaire, *much closer to forgetting than what is usually called memory? And is not this work of spontaneous recollection, in which remembrance is the woof and forgetting the warf, a counterpart to Penelope's work rather than its likeness?"*

This woof and warf of remembrance and forgetting is a dialectic of motion and stasis, of decongealed flow (trans-subjective process, or narrative, or becoming) and its various congealed moments (ontologies, characters, subjects and their plots and analytics), only through and in which our human condition allows us to grasp the processual-real. But we must make sure that we are aware of the fact that what is glimpsed by us in our human condition in those individual and discrete moments is the appearance of the trans-human processual-real at that moment and the trans-subjective, processual logic of the real. Benjamin and, as he shows, Proust are both sanguine on that score:

"Only the actus purus *of recollection itself, not the author or the plot, constitutes the unity of the text. One may even say that the intermittence of author and plot is only the reverse of the continuum of memory, the pattern on the back side of the tapestry."*

The "continuum of memory" and "the tapestry" are allegories of the decongealed, trans-subjective process (recovery of loss) while "the author" and "the plot" are its various moments in which the recovery of the lost processual-real is apprehended, and which in turn congeal to once again produce loss by repressing the processual-real by imprisoning it in its various respective moments, which then present themselves as eternalised ontologies of the real or, in the terms of our discussion here, the ontology of loss. Their "intermittence" is the effect that is produced by the operation to defreeze them in order to recover the lost moments of the real and through them the processuality of the real. This Proustian logic of remembrance, which Benjamin so incisively lays bare, not only constitutes the model of historiography the latter proposes in his 'Theses on the Philosophy of History' (*Illuminations)* but also deeply informs his own memoiristic writings such as 'A Berlin Chronicle' (*Reflections*).

Of course, loss/excess is bound to be (posed as) an ontology. That is so because its coming into being is tied up with the ontology that embodies gain and thereby dialectically originates or founds the constitutive logical horizon of the system (capitalist modernity) that produces this alienated, hierarchical binary of gain and loss. But this ontology of loss not only posits the recovery of what had been lost in ontologised terms due to the repressive manoeuvre of the ontology of gain, it also simultaneously posits the twin logics of autonomous self-expression and processual-real, which are the repressed inverse of the loss-producing, truth-sapping, autonomy-robbing logic of formal determination or representation constitutive of the horizon of capitalist modernity that is co-founded and co-reinforced by the ontology of gain. (The logic of autonomous self-expression – which the capitalist logic of representation, formal determination or symbolisation constitutively precludes – implies the appearance of essence as itself and not through representation or signification by another ontological appearance or sign.) Unless the ontology of recovery (of what had been lost) self-reflexively expresses this awareness of its constitutive logic at all constituent instances of its moment, the politics it would pose would generate, to begin with, a Fascist/Bonapartist tendency that would strengthen the systemic logic of the very historical moment, whose representative ontology it challenges. Or, it could eventually end up reintroducing the capitalist logic of formal determination/representation and alienation into the form of the new historical moment that it had founded through its initial revolutionary impulse of rupturing the historico-logical conjuncture of a loss-producing moment of capitalist modernity to refound the revolutionary logic of autonomous self-expression of the processual-real. The form that manifests this grave philosophical peril of revolutionary politics is Left authoritarianism of, what may be called following the historical characterisation of the degeneration of the French Revolution of 1789, the Thermidor. Stalinism is but one concrete instance of such a thermidorian institutionalisation or congealment of the revolutionary or processual-real.

The bitter truth, however, is that the Stalinist thermidor is the inevitable outcome of revolutionary politics. For, the unavoidable expression of what had been lost as an ontology of recovery or revolution would lead, equally unavoidably, to its congealment. The decisionist question, in the face of such dangerous inevitability, is where should the wager of revolutionary politics lie: on the side of administrative anti-politics as a subjective embodiment of the autocratic thermidor, or on the side of non-revolutionary quietism that forms the subjectivity of perpetual ironising and absolute political agnosticism, or with the critical oppositional subjectivity of the trans-subjective posed against its arrest in the congealed institutionalisation of one of its moments?

For Marxism and its Marxist bearers at any one of its congealed, thermidorian moments the answer to that question should be fairly clear. The only way a Marxism can remain true to its foundational impulse of recovering the perpetually lost processual-real is to oppose the loss-producing Stalinist thermidor even while upholding the revolutionary logic of recovery of autonomous self-expression, and its constitutive logic of trans-subjectivity, whose foundation at a preceding moment has emerged, as is its wont, in the congealed ontology of the Stalinist thermidor. It is this trans-subjective revolutionary logic that Alain Badiou has chosen to call the One or subjective materiality vis-à-vis its determinate and concrete subjective encapsulation and expression at a specific moment of lived history. And the inevitable congealment of the subjective-material One shows up, according to Badiou, as its division into two – the subject (idea) and the object (materiality). This, needless to say, will produce externalised determination (domination/repression) of the latter by the former, and loss. In other words, the absence of critical self-reflexivity would congeal the momentary ontology of the recovery of what had been lost, producing in its turn its own loss and excess. That would imply the return of the capitalist logic of formal determination or representation it had sought to transcend through resistance.

The question, therefore, is does the Marxist discourse on the logic of revolutionary politics provide a theoretical vantage point from where the subjectivity of revolutionary praxis at a moment of recovery of loss indicate an in-advance critique of its inevitable loss-producing reification and thus escape being identified with the Stalinist thermidor that its formal expression is destined to congeal into?

Clearly, the expression of self-reflexive awareness, or its absence, by an ontology of recovery of what had been lost would determine whether that particular ontology of loss or its recovery will be a subjectivity of revolutionary trans-subjectivity; or whether it is, or will be, a congealed ground of reaction within the symbolic logical horizon of capitalist modernity that it would, as a result, reinforce.

This revolutionary self-reflexivity, wherein the subjectivity of recovery of what is lost consciously envisages itself as the expression of the logic of autonomous or sovereign self-expression in opposition to the loss-producing congealed ontology of gain and the historico-logical horizon of capitalist modernity that co-found one another, is in the same movement a subjective momentary expression of the trans-subjective. Such subjectivity, which is aware that it is essentially expressing the trans-subjective logic of the real through its ontologised recovery at one of its infinite moments indicates the provisional nature of its own ontological appearance and consciously anticipates and projects the need to negate its own ontological appearance to save the processual essence that it is an expression of at that moment of its appearance, but which the imminent congealment of this appearance would also inevitably repress and thus lose for another moment. Such self-consciousness of a subjective political position, which is enshrined in the Marxist theory of dialectics as the logic of negation of negation, is what renders it truly revolutionary.

This formulation of negation of negation is, however, impossible without the idea of "real abstraction" in Marx, in whose work, particularly the *Grundrisse*, Marxist thinkers such as Alfred Sohn-Rethel and others have located the idea that abstraction in social life – as opposed to intellectual abstraction that produces thought and knowledge and which is in turn contingent on such "real abstraction" – is the congealment of ontologised expressions of the processual-real at its various respective moments wrought by the capitalist logic of competitive exchange and alienation. But insofar as such congealment is the inevitable outcome of their appearance as sovereign self-expressions of the processual-real in its various specific moments they are also real. (The processual-real is, however, not a priori but is, in turn, constituted and reconstituted dialectically through the dynamic that is unleashed by the production of loss and its consciousness, which is a constitutive contradiction of the symbolic logic of capitalist modernity.)

3

The Psychoanalytic Moment of Revolution

In the context of these twin Marxist ideas of negation of negation and real abstraction, we are probably now better placed to reflect on the import of Jacques Lacan's declaration – in the lecture with which he opened his famous January-June Seminar of 1964 at the Ecole Normale Superieure in Paris, and which has been translated and published under the title 'Excommunication' in *The Four Fundamental Concepts of Psychoanalysis*:

"Personally, I have never regarded myself as a researcher. As Picasso once said, to the shocked surprise of those around him – I do not seek, I find."

"Indeed, there are in the field of so-called scientific research two domains that can quite easily be recognized, that in which one seeks, and that in which one finds."

This assertion, if one were to receive it as a credo of Lacan's intellectual engagement, can easily be read as an attempt by the psychoanalyst-philosopher to refound the twin logical formulations of Marxism – negation of negation and real abstraction – in, what can be called, the psychoanalytic moment of class struggle. The domain of seeking for Lacan is – if we are to understand it in terms of our concern for loss – the perception of the loss of a self as that loss, which is expressed by a psychic state and is produced within the symbolic horizon of human psychology by the logic of repression. This logic emanates from the dominant and conscious self (ego), and is constitutive of the dynamic that produces, according to Freud, the psychological economy of the human conscious and unconscious and its symbolic logical horizon. This loss-producing psychological economy – which has necessitated the emergence of psychoanalysis as both a therapeutic and epistemological protocol – is, we can argue, following some of Freud's socio-psychological writings, especially *Civilization and its Discontents*, the direct outcome of the encounter between human psychology and the social and socialising logics of capitalist modernity.

But this perception of loss in Lacan's domain of seeking, both in psychological and psychoanalytical registers, is an externalised, phenomenological, passive consciousness of loss that is recognised in terms of precisely the same repressive logic that has constitutively produced it within its own symbolic horizon. Such recognition of loss is, both in terms of psychological-affective experience and as objects of psychoanalytic science, registered through socio-psycho- or psycho-pathological symptoms such as neurosis, anxiety and paranoia. It is in the "domain of finding" – which is something Lacan himself appears to emphatically embrace as the determinant of his psychoanalytic praxis, and where there is no seeking within the symbolic – that the real is found. This finding consists in the loss transcending the logic of the symbolic horizon, within and by which it has been actually produced and has phenomenologically known itself as loss, to be transfigured into another by becoming the sovereign self-expression of its own interiority. This, one would argue, would register within the framework of psychoanalysis (both as a therapeutic and epistemological protocol) as the complete obliteration of the already permeable boundary between the analyst and the analysand, and the curing of the analysand through the transfiguration of his sense of psychic loss, registered in terms of the symbolic system of the repressive modern psychological economy that has both produced it and identified it as such, and of which his pathologies are mere symptoms. Such transfiguration of psychic loss and its ontologised consciousness into another renders the latter into its own logical horizon of non-repressive sovereign self-expression and the trans-subjective real glimpsed in that moment of its unfolding.

These two domains of seeking and finding, and the mutually exclusive relationship that Lacan envisages between them, show how the real can express itself at a moment as its own ontology only by negating the symbolic, which is an embodiment of the congealed ontological appearance of the processual real in the preceding moment. And yet by acknowledging the existence of the domain of seeking, which he personally does not prefer, he suggests that seeking is impelled by the distorted consciousness of the real that is produced within and by the symbolic. Considering that the symbolic horizon and its logic of externalised formal determination or representation is constitutively produced through the congealment of the ontological appearance of the real at one of its many moments, Lacan not only indicates that the symbolic is a real abstraction, but also signals the necessity of prospective negation of the ontological form that finds the real at a moment by becoming its sovereign self-expression through the negation of the congealed ontological appearance (symbol) of the preceding moment of the processual-real.

The keen awareness of a determinate and dialectical relationship between the sense of loss and its transfigured other, that Lacan displays by counter-intuitively demarcating the two "scientific domains" of seeking and finding as mutually exclusive and then by stating his own partial preference for the latter, is expressed even more sharply and systemically by the symbolic-imaginary-real triad he constructs. For Lacan, *seeking* or the consciousness of loss as loss is the play of the imaginary within the horizon of the symbolic. What he *finds* is the real; of the imaginary of loss as loss transfiguring itself into another of recovery by becoming the sovereign self-expression of its own internality and generating its own totally self-grounded and self-contained logical horizon of the determinate aleatory by rupturing out of the horizon constituted by the symbolic logic of externalised formal determination and the historical form that embodies that logic at that moment. Real contingency or aleatory materialism, it must be stated here, is possible only through historical determinateness, which precludes externalised determination or representation by congealed ontological appearances of the processual-real at its various other moments.

This transgressive rupture of and with the horizon of the symbolic by the imaginary of loss as loss – which becomes another because that antithetical imaginary of loss is only possible constitutively within the logical horizon of the symbolic whereby it is produced and known as such – results in the collapse of the contradictorily binarised dyad of the symbolic and the imaginary, and the logic of ontological fixities and formal determination that has been constitutive of this peculiar dyadic relationship. It is the appearance of this moment of the collapse of the dyad that is the real, which offers an evanescent glimpse of its processual nature in that one among its multiple moments and posits a different synthetic horizon of, what in Badiou's words is, the singular-universal where logic or essence is its own form. Or rather, the multitudinous lifeworld of the human beings is its own system and its logic.

When he shuns the domain of seeking for that of finding, Lacan is acting as an engaged militant in the psychoanalytic moment and is essentially envisaging the imaginary, which he rightly sees as a constitutive contradiction produced by the symbolic within its own horizon, as the bearer of the immanently inverse tendency of the counter-symbolic that he seeks to express by turning the imaginary into its own founding ground and its own regulative-logical horizon, thereby bursting open the conjuncture and continuum of the symbolic system to reclaim the real and its processual essence at that particular historico-temporal moment of psychoanalysis.

4

The Free Self:
Pseudo-Recovery or What?

This dialectical and revolutionary Lacanian awareness can be discerned, albeit in a passive mode, in 'psychotic' Portuguese poet Fernando Pessoa's only novel, *The Book of Disquiet*, which Bernardo Soares, one of Pessoa's many heteronyms, wrote as a loose-leaf, meditative journal. Pessoa (or Soares) laments the impossibility of the artist to free himself through his art from the distortionary determinations that life imposes on him, his sovereignty and his autonomous self-expression. According to the poet, the artistic quest for freedom (or recovery of what is lost because of the distortionary repression effected by the symbolic logic constitutive of Pessoa's, and even Soares's, empirically actual history of capitalist modernity) has its locus in the self of the artist, who is constitutively produced with his sense of loss within and by the symbolic logical horizon of life (capitalist modernity).

"And if the office in the Rua dos Douradores represents Life for me, the second floor room I live in on that same street represents Art. Yes, Art, living on the same street as Life but in a different room; Art, which offers relief from life without actually relieving one of living, and which is as monotonous as life itself without actually relieving one of living, and which is as monotonous as life itself but in a different way."

As a consequence, any attempt by that unfree, loss-bearing self to seek freedom for itself, or express that loss through art, would only serve to consolidate the symbolic horizon within which the empirically actual fact of loss and its artistic consciousness are produced. That would, if anything, mean the continuance of both unfreedom and loss.

Although Pessoa himself did nothing in his actually lived empirical life to transfigure his passive consciousness of loss and the art through which he expressed that loss into another, by transgressing the symbolic horizon of his actually lived history within which that loss, its consciousness embodied by his poet's ontology and the art that emanated from that ontology as its consciousness, took shape, he was acutely aware of the need to do so and said as much. That is precisely why he terms the self's questing after freedom as an act of "cowardly love" since it ends up consolidating the loss-producing symbolic horizon that enframes this loss and its ontological expression.

"Slavery is the only law of life, there is no other, because this law must be obeyed; there is no possible rebellion against it or refuge from it. Some are born slaves, some become slaves, some have slavery *thrust upon them. The cowardly love we all have of freedom – which if it were given to us we would all repudiate as being too new and strange – is the irrefutable proof of how our slavery weighs upon us. Even I, who have just expressed my desire to have a hut or a cave where I could be free from the monotony of being myself, would I really dare to go off to this hut or cave, knowing and understanding that, since the monotony exists in me alone, I would never be free of it? Suffocating where I am, would I breathe any better there when it is my lungs that are diseased and not the air about me? Who is to say I, longing out loud for the pure sun and the open fields, for the bright sea and the wide horizon, would not miss my bed, or my meals, or having to go down eight flights of stairs to the street, or dropping in at the tobacconist's on the corner, or saying good morning to the barber standing idly by?"*

"Everything that surrounds us becomes part of us, it seeps into us with every experience of the flesh and of life and, like the web of the great Spider, binds us subtly to what is near, ensnares us in a fragile cradle of slow death, where we lie rocking in the wind."

The reason why Pessoa was probably loath to make this transfiguring leap from the artistic (embodying passive consciousness of loss) to the political (active consciousness of loss by which loss ceases to be loss) is because he failed to fully realise the political implications of his art-destroying poetic enunciations. Pessoa did not, unlike Lacan, or the latter's favourite poet Rimbaud, envisage the aesthetic register as the self expressing in a cellular form an entirely new counter-juridical order and unalienated, self-determined/free associative historico-logical epoch that posits its own founding by rupturing through and with the historico-logical conjuncture of actually lived history of capitalist modernity. He saw the aesthetic for what it was – an ontology of contradiction that is constitutively produced within and by the symbolic horizon of actually lived history – but no more. He proved unwilling, or at any rate incapable, of strategically re-signifying such a contradictory ontology in terms of the counter-logical tendency – to the constitutive alienating, representational and competitive logic of the symbolic system of capitalist modernity – that is immanent in such ontologies of contradiction.

5

The Symbolic Economy of Aesthetics: A Coopted Tale

Following Lacan's renewal of the classically radical Hegelian-Marxist triadic and recursive dialectic of thesis-antithesis-synthesis as symbolic-imaginary-real in his psychoanalytic moment, we would do well to see some artistic-literary practices and experiments in terms of whether or not they re-envisage the aesthetic deportment – present as constitutive contradiction within the horizon of the symbolic system as a register for expressing loss and/or its sense – as a cellular form of the inversely oppositional or critical logic immanent in that system.

We should recall that the thesis (or the Lacanian symbolic) is the objectifying logical horizon of empirically actual life in all its various momentary ramifications. The antithesis (or the Lacanian imaginary) is the constitutive contradiction of the thesis produced by the symbolic logic that the thesis founds and helms. The synthesis (or the Lacanian Real) – which is a new self-grounded, self-determined horizon of the One without any two – is, therefore, absolutely sovereign and completely free of conflicts and contradictions. This is the horizon of inverse opposition, critique and politics, vis-à-vis the qualitatively different symbolic spatio-temporality of administrative anti-politics and competing ontologised fixities. The synthesis, however, is immanent in the antithesis's ontology of contradiction and is always posed, either actively or potentially, by it. The revolutionary Lacanian operation, mentioned earlier, of turning the imaginary into its own founding ground and its own regulative-logical horizon, is the active recognition of necessity in the antithesis and the constant attempt to make the leap to the qualitatively different synthetic horizon that such recognition posits.

All contradictory registers of antithesis, produced and signified within and by the quasi-objective logical horizon of the historically determinate symbolic system, are constitutive of that system. But in studying them retrospectively in and through their effects and traces, to figure out the constitutive logic they expressed in their evental moment of enunciation or production, some can be seen to have a more critical and sovereignty-seeking orientation towards their respective theses and their respective symbolic horizons, within which they were all produced, than the others. In fact, this quantitative difference among various registers has, at times, shown up as a fundamental qualitative break.

Muktibodh's poem 'Bramharakshas', thanks to it being imbued most acutely with the poet's perfect grasp of the triadic dialectic, is one of those rare examples of an artistic-literary production that very self-consciously founds itself as the ground of the synthetic even as it expresses the self-reflexive critique of art in whose determinate moment it re-enacts Badiou and Slavoj Žižek's invariant communist logic of sovereign self-expression and the processual-real. Words, Muktibodh shows and we must see like he wanted his readers to see, can become their own flesh.

The estrangement and loneliness that the symbolic system visits on Bramharakshas because of his intellectual arrogance and disdain for the system this arrogance produces in him, and which in turn impels him to court such marginalisation and atomised loneliness with even more arrogant rage, is etched out rather poignantly by Muktibodh as the lot of anti-systemic intellectuals, who, given that they persevere with their 'unproductive' intellectual pursuits in the face of socio-economic marginalisation that the culture industry of the symbolic system of capitalist modernity and its concomitant societal norms impose on them and their pursuits, are the perfect ontological embodiments of the consciousness of loss as such. Something that Muktibodh captures in the invective-ridden, lamenting tone of Bramharakshas by giving a descriptive account of it.

Bawdi kee un ghani gaharahiyon may shunya
Bramharakshas ek paitha hai,
va bheetar se umardti gunj kee bhi gunj,
bardbardahat-shabd pagal se.
Gahan anumanita
tan kee malinta
door karne ke liye pratipal
paap-chchaya door karne ke liye, din-raath
swachch karne –
Bramharakshas
ghis raha hai deh
haath ke panje, baraabar
banh-chchati-muh chchapaachchap
khoob karte saaf,
phir bhi mael
phir bhi mael!!

Aur. honthon se
anokha strotra, koi kruddh mantrochchar,
athva shundh Sanskrit galiyon ka jwar,
mastak kee lakiren
bun rahin
alochanayon kay chamakte tar!!
Us akhand snan ka pagal pravah...
pran may samvedna hai syah!!

(In the emptiness of the deep dark depths of the pond/ lies a Bramharakshas,/ And an echo of the echo bursting out from the inside,/ like the words of an insane mutter./ To rid himself, every moment, of grave doubts and his body of its squalid griminess / To rid himself of his sinful shadow/ To cleanse himself/ The Brahmarakshas scrubs his body, day and night without any respite./ His paws moving continuously over his arms-chest-face. splash! Splash! Splash!/ To rub himself clean, absolutely clean,/ Yet there's dirt/ Yet there's grime!!

And. from his lips emanate bizarre shlokas, like some angry enunciation of spells,/ or else, a torrent of invectives in impeccable Sanskrit,/ the lines on his forehead/ knitting together/ shimmering threads of criticisms!!/ The insane flow of that unceasing bath. /. the blackness of his sensitive soul!!) (My translation.)

But, the poet, even as he hails Bramharakshas's dogged pursuit of 'useless' knowledge as much as the status of the lonely marginal that such a pursuit is bound to bring, rues his failure – precisely on account of the same intellectual arrogance that had given Bramharakshas the courage to court systemic rejection unto death – to actively and critically engage with the system in order to transform it while simultaneously transforming his own loss-bearing ontology.

Kintu yug badla va aaya keerti-vyavsayi
...labhkari karya-me se dhan,
va dhan may se hriday-man,
aur, dhan-abhibhoot antahkaran may se
satya kee jhain
nirantar chilchilatee thi.
Atmachetas kintu is
vyaktitva may thi pranmai anban...
vishwachetas be-banav!!
Mahatta ke charan may tha
vishadakul man!
Mera usi se un dinon hota Milan yadi
toh vyatha uski swyam jeekar
batataa mai usey uska swyam ka mulya
uskee mahatta!
Va us mahatta ka
hum sareekhon ke liye upyog,
us aantarikta ka batataa mai mahatva!!

Pis gaya vah bheetree
au' baharee doh kathin paton beech,
aisee tragedy hai neech!!

(But the epoch changed, and traders of fame arrived/ ...in profitable activity shimmered wealth,/ while only in that wealth could heart-and-mind be glimpsed,/ and, the brightness of truth flashed

unceasingly from the inner recesses of a soul overwhelmed by such riches./ But in this self-conscious/ being resided life-affirming contradictions.../ an unreconstructed consciousness of the world!! On the feet of greatness lay prostrate/ a despairing soul!/ If only I had met with him then/ I would surely have lived his pain/ to tell him his worth/ his greatness!

Also, the use such greatness could be put to/ for people like us,/ And the significance of such inwardness I would surely have communicated to him!!/ But alas, it ended in a lowly tragedy!/ Caught as he was between the inner and outer mill stones of his dilemma that ground him to dust!!) (My translation.)

After all, the marginalisation that the symbolic system of capitalist modernity visits on an intransigent intellectual such as Bramharakshas can be construed, as is actually done by him in the poem, as capitalist society's gift of seclusion and awe. That the vampire-like symbolic system of capitalist modernity can, and does, enable its most intransigent rejectors such as Bramharakshas to draw such false comfort, shows how this real-symbolic system can differentially include and thereby distort even the anti-capitalist symbolic economy of non-exchange, embodied by such uncompromising bearers of the sense of loss as Bramharakshas, into a commodity and ideology of the marginal's pride in maintaining himself as a marginal.

Kintu, gahri bawdi
kee bheetree deewar per
tirchi giree Ravi-rashmi
ke udte huye parmanu, jab
tal tak pahunchte hain kabhi
tab Bramharakshas samajhta hai, Surya nay
jhukkar 'Namaste' kar diya.
Path bhoolkar jab chandni
kee kiran takraye kahin deewar per,
tab Bramharakshas samajhta hai
vandana kee chandni nay
gyan-guru maanaa usey.

(But, when and if some stray atoms of the sunbeam,/ which falls

slantedly on the inner walls that enclose the deep pond,/ reach its bottom/ Bramharakshas takes that to be the Sun's wish to bow before him in obeisance./ If ever moonlight, straying from its path,/ collides with those walls,/ Bramharakshas is given to believe that the Moon,/ which has accepted him as its master,/ is singing paeans to him.) (My translation.)

This problem cannot, clearly, be overcome unless that symbolic economy is transformed into its own political-economic ground or flesh through an active oppositional and transformative engagement with the symbolic system of capitalist modernity and its constitutive logic of competition, alienation and externalised formal determination or representation.

It is this unfinished task of Bramharakshas that the poet promises, towards the end of the poem, to take up and accomplish. But not before he has vowed to do so as "the truest disciple of Bramharakshas" without whose (passive) consciousness of loss determinate, and thus effective, resistance would not be possible.

Vah jyoti anjaani sada ko so gayee
yah kyon hua!
Kyon yah hua!!
Mai Bramharakshas ka sajal-ur shishya
hona chahta
jisse ki uska adhoora karya,
uskee vedna ka srot
sangat, purna nishkarshon talak
pahuncha sakoon.

(That light has been snuffed out for ever/ Why! Oh why! Did this have to happen!/ I now wish to become/ the truest disciple of Bramharakshas/ so that I can take his unfinished task,/ the source of his pain,/ closer to its deserving conclusions.) (My translation.)

This returns us to the beginning where one had contended that revolutionary resistance is not possible without a consciousness or recognition of loss as loss.

The problematic that Muktibodh expounds in 'Bramharakshas' with regard to the location of the aesthetic register in the triadic dialectic of the symbolic-imaginary-real is taken up with as much critical sharpness, vis-à-vis the traditional Indic philosophico-spiritual imaginary, by Hazariprasad Dwivedi in his novel *Anaamdas ka Potha* (The Treatise of the Unnamed One). Dwivedi, who unlike Muktibodh, was neither a Marxist nor an avant-garde litterateur but a rather traditional writer, albeit in modern Hindi literature, displays a sharply intuitive grasp of the operation of this triadic dialectic as the author of *Anaamdas*.... He, through his astute plotting of the novel as a critique of renunciation in its linkages with the institutionalised Brahminism and Brahminical knowledge production in post-Independence India, ends up envisaging the philosophico-spiritual register as a cellular form in the self of the renunciant – located within the symbolic horizon of what such an all-renouncing philosopher-hermit deems as the illusory 'this-world' – of a qualitatively and logically different historical time.

Raikwa Tapaskumar, the protagonist of the novel, is a young ascetic, whose choice to be a renunciant makes him into an ontological embodiment of the loss of truth in the 'illusory this-world' of his empirically actual historical era of the *Chhandogya Upanishad*. But he realises he cannot go into Samadhi as he is assailed by the misery of the starving and the poor. On his mother's suggestion, Tapaskumar gives up his ascetic life to plunge into 'this-world' as a householder. *Anaamdas*...is neither meant to be – as it would appear from the rather sketchy summary of its plot provided here – a simple-minded criticism of renunciation as escapism nor its rejection for the empirical actuality of life in 'this-world'. Instead, it shows how the philosophico-spiritual being of an Upanishadic ascetic or hermit, if it fails to actively work towards materially realising another new historico-logical horizon of human life that it posits vis-à-vis the empirical actuality of life within the symbolic horizon of the 'this-worldly', will end up consolidating its own ascetic ontology and the symbolic system that he calls the illusory this-world, and within which he is situated as a conscious ontological bearer of all that has been lost in the illusions of 'this-world'.

6

Loss As Resistance:
A New Constellation of Revolution

The transfiguration of the passive consciousness of loss and its constitutive ontology into an actively engaged consciousness and ontology of resistance is very clearly articulated in a linocut (*Flood*) from the atelier of revolutionary Bengali artist Chhitaprasad. The work (circa 1947) depicts a pauperised peasant family of Bengal wading through flood waters towards dry land, away from their home and hearth, which have been destroyed by the deluge. We see a woman and a young girl in the peasant group looking back with despair at their marooned and half-destroyed house even as a man looks up at the overcast sky, while trying to shelter a young boy with his emaciated arms, fearing more elemental fury. But at the head of the group is a man, who is walking towards the shore with his fists clenched and face taut with an angry determination to struggle against nature's fury and possibly also the systemic socio-political condition that has rendered him and his poor family vulnerable to such fury.

In this Chhittaprasad we see how the affect, consciousness and the ontologies of loss, which in the absence of the angry man at the head of the group would have continued to be situated within their empirically given history and time of the symbolic system of capitalism, have because of him been transfigured to become part of a new historical constellation of resistance against such empirical history and the symbolic system of capitalism that has generated it.

A similar reconfiguring of an empirically given history of loss – within the horizon of the symbolic system of capitalist modernity – into another spatio-temporality and logicality of resistance that seeks to found itself by disrupting the given conjunctural logic of symbolic determination and loss, is seen in filmmaker Mrinal Sen's *Calcutta 71*. The syntagmatic units that constitute the narrative of the film are four disparate short stories of loss in the city of Calcutta through the '30s, '40s, '50s and '60s. The first centres on the tenuous living quarters of a petty-bourgeois family facing pauperisation. Its home is eventually destroyed by rain displacing the family into a common shelter levelling, in the process, the remaining culturally-ordained fragile class boundaries between the underclass and the lower-middle class. The second story is about a young woman from a *bhadralok* ('respectable' middle-class) family – living in *chawl*-like conditions in the city after being displaced from its village by the great famine – being ambivalently egged into prostitution by her own mother to support the family. The next one revolves around the lives of poor, rural and suburban teenagers, who rebel against existing food-control laws to smuggle rice into the city in order to earn their livelihood under difficult economic conditions. Last but not least is a tale of disengaged intellectual voyeurism and ritual philanthropy by a corrupt and self-aggrandising Calcutta bourgeoisie amid the hunger and social disturbances brought about by the violent assertion of the lumpen-proletariat, uprooted from their rural homes by the socio-economic processes that constituted, what in canonised national history is called, nation building.

But what unifies these discrete units into a single narrative syntax, even as they are bound together into a singular paradigmatic relationship, is the dénouement the filmmaker has plotted for them. The four stories eventually culminate in the rupture of the horizon of empirically actual capitalist history of those four Calcuttas, within which they had been produced and perceived as loss, to found the real Calcutta of 1971 of young communist and naxal revolutionaries bursting out on to its streets to mostly become martyrs in fake encounter killings. Through this reconfiguration of four Calcuttas of lost denizens into a Calcutta of revolution, Sen shows us how concrete, empirical instances of loss can be seen, in a transfigured optic, not as part of the history that produces such loss and maintains it as such, but as constituent units of a new historical constellation of revolutionary resistance.

But this ontological expression of the real, whereby the real becomes its own appearance (symbol), would, as we have seen, inevitably lead to its congealment, producing its own loss and excess. We have also discussed how the self-reflexive deployment of the Marxist idea of negation of negation saves the trans-subjective politics of resistance from being obstructed, repressed and distorted by the congealed ontologies through which it appears at its various moments. The question, specifically with regard to art as a historico-logical moment — where the subjectivity of loss is also often transfigured in a determinate way into a subjectivity of resistance – is what are the works and practices of art that have deployed this self-reflexive Marxist idea of negation of negation while seeking to reconstitute the subjectivity of loss into a subjectivity of recovery and/or resistance.

7

An Unlikely Communist Hero

The self-reflexive sensibility of negation of negation has been an integral, prominent and, often, overt part of the works and practices of many avant-garde artists and writers, who have either been part of the international working-class movement or closely aligned to it. But one's caprice compels one to look for this sensibility elsewhere: in a poet, whose life, work and death have come to constitute an emblematic reminder of the horrors of Stalinism and, as many would argue, the revolutionary politics of the working class.

My warmth, my exhalation, one can already see
On the window-pane of eternity.

The pattern printed in my breathing here
Has not been seen before.

Let the moment's condensation vanish without trace:
The cherished pattern no one can efface.

These lines from Osip Mandelshtam's 1909 poem (8) from *Stone* make for a precisely beautiful example of recovery and affirmation of the self's absolute sovereignty at a moment through the negation of what had repressed it (*The pattern printed in my breathing here/ Has not been seen before.*), even while indicating almost concurrently the necessity to negate the momentary form/appearance of this recovery. This is nothing else but Mandelshtam's way of attempting to prevent or preempt the recurrence of loss – something the repressive operation of that appearance would inevitably produce at the next instant — that he has recovered through transfiguration. Mandelshtam is in no doubt that this proposed negation of the momentary appearance of absolute sovereignty of the self would spell the reclamation of the same essence that had been recovered at a prior moment through the emergence of the appearance that is now sought to be negated (*Let the moment's condensation vanish without trace:/ The cherished pattern no one can efface.*)

But this decision to take Osip Mandelshtam as an illustration of the self-reflexive play of the idea of negation of negation in art is, on second thoughts, not a caprice after all. Among other things, it is an attempt to free his poetry from a reading that is tinted by an optic of despair, precisely the sensibility his poetic vision expressly broke with, but which has been imposed on his poetry by many of his 'ardent' admirers, who in deciding to be moved much less by the artistic expression of his personal experience of life-wrenching loss than by his actual plight, have subordinated, unwittingly or otherwise, the former to the latter. That, needless to say, has done great disservice to his poetry and the larger aesthetic sensibility that underpins it, beside, of course, delivering a liberalist body blow to the entire legacy of working-class politics by identifying it completely with the various thermidorian episodes to one of which our poet fell a gratuitous victim. My concern has been to show how Mandelshtam provides us with a ground, not for the liberalist anti-Stalinism of lamenting and decrying the Stalinist horrors he experienced, but for a genuinely transgressive and revolutionary critique of Stalinist congealment and repression of working-class politics.

Osip Mandelshtam's break with the lamenting mode of accounting for loss becomes even more sharply evident when we see it in juxtaposition with his wife Nadzheda Mandelshtam's testimonial response to the Stalinist horrors, an experience they both shared, in her two-part memoirs titled *Hope Against Hope* and *Hope Abandoned*. There can be absolutely no dispute that the two-part memoirs, especially the first, constitutes one of the most poignantly brilliant and beautiful works of testimonial writing in the canon and annals of world literature. The comparison that one seeks to make between the husband and the wife is, therefore, not an attempt to diminish the literary-artistic power of the *Hope...* books. Neither should it be seen as an attempt to understate the horrors of Stalinism or trivialise the experiences the Mandelshtams and their friends had to undergo, and which she recounts with such sharp beauty in those books by her. My only intention here today is to show how her choice to take recourse to the testimonial mode in order to engage with the horrific empirical actuality of everyday life in Stalin's USSR bespeaks a sensibility and consciousness that is oriented towards experiencing and expressing repression and loss as loss in an externalised, phenomenological fashion, even as her husband chooses to encounter and express the same experiences in a fashion that transfigures them into another. True, the few Osip Mandelshtam poems we discuss here to illustrate this contrast between the sensibilities of the husband and the wife are all from before 1917. But the fact of the matter is that Mandelshtam's transfiguring expression of loss is something that continued, with a few perfectly legitimate exceptions, to be the dominant and even salient feature of his poetic sensibility and diction even in the darkest days of his life in Soviet Union.

The tone, register and style of his poems are marked by an absence of, what in Nietzsche is termed, *"ressentiment"* (reactivity/revenge). Nadzheda experienced and articulated repression and loss as lament, pain and despair, which shows that she knew loss only as such, congealed and thereby as a contradictory (or direct) opposite of gain/victory that founds the symbolic system of (state) capitalist modernity which encompasses such loss as its constitutive element and thus precludes the possibility for the passive ontological bearers (objects) of such loss to overcome the externalised, phenomenological paraphernalia imposed on them by the symbolic system within which their loss is produced. The same repression and loss are, in Osip's case, transfigured into a *really* possible world of joyful life and recovery even as it evokes a fleeting pain – qualitatively (not merely quantitatively) different from the actual intense pain born out of his and Nadzheda's suffering from the empirically actual fact of repression and loss — of the *really* possible world having still not been *actualised*. This transfigured register or subjectivity of loss as recovery is, in contrast to the subjectivity of loss as contradictory (direct) opposite to the ontology of gain, ranged in non-contradictory (logically inverse) opposition to the so-called ontology of gain and the symbolic system it has founded and it helms. Through his transfigured subjectivity of loss as another, Osip Mandelshtam indicates that the consciousness of recovery of what has been lost has to be much more than the ontologised recovery of that loss at any given moment.

The poet's transfigured subjectivity of loss as another is evident in the defamaliarisation, vis-à-vis his empirically lived history, that he produces by presenting other *strangely* possible worlds in his poems. Worlds that he inhabits with a joy that finds no correlate in the joy that could be actually experienced, was actually experienced, by the powerful of his empirically actual historical time. This is a surreal joy, an empirically impossible joy, a joy that is fleeting in its materiality in his, and our, mind, soul and flesh. We could call this the joy of spectral materiality, in that the material ground of such joy is real like an apparition, which is not the same thing as illusory. A fitting example could be the 1908 poem (4) from *Stone*:

To read only children's books, treasure
Only childish thoughts, throw
Grown-up things away
And rise from deep sorrows.

I'm tired to death of life,
I accept nothing it can give me,
But I love my poor earth
Because it's the only one I've seen.

In a far-off garden I swung
On a simple wooden swing,
And I remember dark tall firs
In a hazy fever.

As for the register of lament, not only does Osip Mandelshtam criticise and reject it, he depicts this affect of his empirically actual history, through a kind of dialectical reversal, as uncanny in and alien to the world of his poetry. 'The Lutheran' (1912) from *Stone* is a case in point:

On a walk I came across a funeral
Near the Lutheran church, last Sunday.
An absentminded passer-by, I stopped to watch
The rigorous distress on the faces of the flock.

I couldn't make out what language they were speaking,
And nothing shone except fine brass
And reflections from the lazy horse-shoes
On the toneless Sunday side-roads.

In the resilient half-light of the carriage
Where sadness, the dissembler, lay entombed,
Wordless and tearless and chary of greetings
A buttonhole of autumn roses gleamed.

The foreigners stretched out in a black ribbon
And weeping ladies went on foot,
Red faces veiled; while, above them,
Nothing stopped the stubborn coachman.

Whoever you were, Lutheran deceased,
They buried you with ease and artlessness
Eyes were dimmed with the decency of tears,
Bells rang out with dignified restraint.

I thought – no need for speeches:
We are not prophets nor precursors,
We do not delight in heaven nor live in fear of hell,
In dull noon we burn like candles.

The poet Mandelshtam encounters the rituals of loss, death and grieving as if he were a denizen of a world to which all this is unfamiliar, alien even. (*I couldn't make out what language they were speaking,/ And nothing shone except fine brass/ And reflections from the lazy horse-shoes/ On the toneless Sunday side-roads.*) In his poetic world, which is implicitly and obliquely posited here in the poem through its embodiment in the poet, we sense a new norm of life and a new structure of history "where sadness" is a "dissembler" that presumably falsifies the expression of loss by manifesting it as such. It is a new space to which the language of lament or grief does not belong (*I couldn't make out what language they were speaking,..*), even as the awareness of the pain of loss and loss as such in empirical actuality seethes just below the surface of that world and its consciousness. For, how else does one explain the poet's expressed awareness that a funeral embodies loss. And yet what he finds troubling in the funereal ambience is the absolutisation of death or loss that completely precludes the transgression of the symbolic horizon of life (or gain) that founds itself through the constitution of contradictory and mutually alienated binaries of life (gain) and death (loss). (*I thought – no need for speeches:/ We are not prophets nor precursors,/ We do not delight in heaven nor live in fear of hell,/ In dull noon we burn like candles.*)

This consciousness of transfigured loss in Osip Mandelshtam is a dialectical sensibility that leads simultaneously to the consciousness of transfigured life, whereby every ontological death or loss is the possibility, even necessity, for the emergence of a new ontological life or gain. So with every death occurs a new life, which is the recovery of the processual-real or the trans-subjective becoming from the congealed ontological appearance of its prior moment. Thus the death of an ontology of a moment becomes the condition for the resurrection or re-enactment of the processual-real at the next moment, through the emergence of another momentarily real and momentarily provisional ontology.

8

No History Without Loss: Poetic Lessons from Nature

The absolutisation of the consciousness of death/loss that leads to the consolidation of the constitutive logic of the symbolic system – which is founded through the reification of life/gain, even as that produces its constitutive contradiction in the reified idea or ontology of death/loss – obviates the transfiguration of death/loss into a new life. It thus stymies the possibility of recovery of a new processual, trans-human (read trans-ontological) logic of life. Bishnu Dey's poem 'Sandiper Char' critiques this absolutisation of the consciousness of death/loss precisely in those terms:

Prakritir maya
Aha banorajinila!
Hey tamaltalibon!
Sumdrobijonsikta shofen kallol!
Baaliyaardi hira jaley choto choto tila,
Shanto mridu khardi – Jeno tanukaya
Ashtadashi! Prakritir maya –
Jibanmaraney gantha jibaner ayushmanroopey
Katey na ebar chchuti
Sacchal bhushargo sukhey – kobey chupey chupey
Hoye geche jibaner haar –
Aajke shobai pratibeshi bhai, hey prakriti, bhuley jai
Jibaner maraner haarey bandha jibaner chchobi
Aaj shudhu maari, mari, purdi o purdai, khepi ar luti.

Eh maraney pran nai, eh toh nesha unmaader,
Shaktimadamatta andho pagaler apraakrito aandhi!
Hey prakriti aamra manush, ai maransaader madiraye
Aamrai kobi, noi talibon
Sari sari talsuparir
Samudrabijonsnigdha dhaiuer jiban noi, — chchya dhaka khardi
Noi, hirajala baaliyaardi noi, hey prakriti,
Aamrai mari aaj aapan pashar chchakey
Tobu sthir jani, tobu man drido satye bandhi

Ai rogey eh maraney, praan naaye, shaman sujogey
Nikaote sudurey Kashmire o Tribancurey raktakta Golden Rockeey
Anek Hasnabadey praner aabaadey, noye buniyaadi hatho apaghath,
Hey Prakriti aamra manush, noi bonorajinil talibon tatorekha noi –
Aamaderi karme lekha aamader durgata jiban
Aamaderi bhabbishath o srimti.

Dey contrasts the absolutised consciousness of death in human life, as a dominant conception of life and death in capitalist modernity, with the more liberatory and productive notion of death as it obtains in nature, where death/decays is a necessary possibility for new life and its continuance as a process.

...Jibanmaraney gantha jibaner ayushmanroopey
Katey na ebar chchuti
Sacchal bhushargo sukhey – kobey chupey chupey
Hoye geche jibaner haar –
Aajke shobai pratibeshi bhai, hey prakriti, bhuley jai
Jibaner maraner haarey bandha jibaner chchobi
Aaj shudhu maari, mari, purdi o purdai, khepi ar luti.

A maraney pran nai, a toh nesha unmaader,
Shaktimadamatta andho pagaler apraakrito aandhi!
Hey prakriti aamra manush, ai maransaader madiraye
Aamrai kobi, noi talibon
Sari sari talsuparir
Samudrabijonsnigdha dhaiuer jiban noi, — chchya dhaka khardi

Noi, hirajala baaliyaardi noi, hey prakriti,
Aamrai mari aaj aapan pashar chchakey
Tobu sthir jani, tobu man drido satye bandhi…

(*The immortal form of life woven in the garland of life and death will not suffice this time during the period of repose. One does not know when — in this tranquil earthly heaven – life was surreptitiously defeated. Oh nature I forget that everybody is a neighbour, brother. Life's picture today is enframed in life and its death.*

Today, we kill, die, burn and be burnt, and embark on enraged plunder.

In this death there is no life. This is the intoxication of insanity. The storm of fury of a blind man drunk on power. Oh nature we are humans, poets drunk on the wine of death. We are not a palm forest, or rows and rows of areca nut palms. We are not the life of sea-calmed waves — or a delta under a shade. We are not the sandy plains sparkling with the glow of diamonds. Oh nature, we die today caught in our own moves on our own chessboard. Yet, we are so sure. Yet, we are so certain about the truth..). (Translation mine.)

From here we gather that within the horizon of the unalienated, processual-real, for which nature is a metaphor in Dey, not only does the death (loss) of an ontological appearance lead to a new ontology of life but is the necessary condition for the recovery of the future of the processual-real, which would otherwise not emerge from the repressive signification of its prior congealed appearances and, thus, be lost. Russian poet Arseny Tarkovsky in 'Objects' (from *Life, Life*) envisages death in terms of the dissolution or loss of an ontological fixity or self and deems it necessary. In this poem we see how he completely realises Osip Mandelshtam's poetic vision of loss of the past becoming a loss of the future. And how the subjective operation of recovery transforms loss into not what we have been dispossessed of in the past but, because of that, what we are losing out by way of the unemerged future. Here we see in the subjectivity of recovery of loss a collapse of temporal linearity, and the flow of time as a question constitutively contingent on the founding of a different plane, a different vector of history.

Objects which shared my childhood
Keep on disappearing:
Lighting lamps and black gunpowder,
Dark water from the well,

Plush red divans and decadent-
Framed Islands of the dead,
Men with moustaches, old photographs,
Aeroplanes made out of reeds,

Nadson's consumptive three-parters,
Adonis-like lawyers in morning coats,
The peculiar smell of galoshes,
Shoulders sloping from ostrich-like necks,

The curlicues of drunken symbolists,
Platitudes of strapping futurists,
Slogans on lime and chestnut trees,
Gangsters' imbecilic shotguns,

The hard sign and the letter yat –
One disappeared, the other altered –
And where there never used to be a comma
Now death intervenes as well.

I've done so little for the future,
Though the future's all I crave.
I don't want to start all over again
As if I've been wasting my time.

But there's no guarantee
I can play with the modern inventions –
I'm stepping on my grandson's baubles,
My great-grandson's glory.

The craving for the future is, in Arseny Tarkovsky, the craving of the processual-real that expressed itself through the ontological appearance of the poet's self to emerge sovereign at the moment of the poet's self – *I've done so little for.the future,/Though the future's all I crave./ I don't want to start all over again/ As if I've been wasting my time* – even as that self or ontology rues the fact that it has done "so little for (that) future" precisely because its congealed appearance has repressed that future and prevented it from emerging as its sovereign self-expression.

And, therefore, this processual-real, which is what the poet's self expressed at one of its moments, can only really get to its real future if that self (ontological appearance) of the poet gets out of the way. (*But there's no guarantee/ I can play with the modern inventions –/ I'm stepping on my grandson's baubles,/ My great-grandson's glory.*)

9

Future is Forever, Or How Not to Regain Lost Time

Therefore, what is lost and experienced as loss in the present is in the past but what can be recovered in trying to truly reclaim that loss in the present is the future. The recovery of loss ontologised as the past would be a pyrrhic, pseudo recovery as it would entail recovery through gaining or winning, thereby producing loss yet again. The idea of recovering, rather reclaiming, what is lost would be truly revolutionary when it recovers the condition of not losing, something that is lost in losing. In other words, the loss ontologised as the past is the constitutive contradiction of the symbolic system of capitalist modernity that is dialectically co-founded and helmed by the ontology of gain. Any attempt to recover that past-ised ontology of loss would be an effort constitutively confined within the logical horizon of the symbolic system of capitalist modernity, which can be called life, society or what have you, and would only end up reinforcing the symbolic system. The idea is to reclaim the logical horizon where there is no loss because there is no gain. That is precisely the reason why Marx's scientific socialism, even as it critiques the founding of capitalism through expropriation of some pre-capitalist producers by others (primitive accumulation of capital), does not strive to restore pre-capitalist communitarianism. Rather, it is a battle for the reclamation of a new horizon where capital with its founding ontology of gain disappears together with the nowproletarianised-then-pre-capitalist artisans and peasants, who as ontological bearers of loss are its constitutive contradiction.

But the human condition, as we have seen earlier, allows us to reclaim the processual-real only in its momentary ontologised appearances. In such a situation, production of loss through congealment would be a permanent affair as, therefore, should be recovery. Clearly, the reclamation of the processual-real or the future is a perpetually infinite becoming. That is reason enough to end for now with the prescient words of Louis Althusser: "Future lasts a long time."